Smithsonian

THE EMANCIPATION PROCLAMATION INKSTAND

What an Artifact Can Tell Us About the **Historic Document**

by Jehan Jones-Radgowski

CAPSTONE PRESS
a capstone imprint

Capstone Captivate is published by Capstone Press,
an imprint of Capstone.
1710 Roe Crest Drive
North Mankato, Minnesota 56003
www.capstonepub.com

Library of Congress Cataloging-in-Publication Data is available on the Library of Congress website.

ISBN: 978-1-4966-9577-2 (hardcover)
ISBN: 978-1-4966-9681-6 (paperback)
ISBN: 978-1-9771-5501-6 (eBook PDF)

Summary: With the stroke of a pen, President Abraham Lincoln freed the slaves. Or did he? Who did the Emancipation Proclamation really free? And what became of the inkstand on which he wrote it? Find answers to these questions, and learn what an artifact can tell us about history.

Image Credits
Alamy: Historical Images Archive, cover (left); Collection of the Smithsonian National Museum of African American History and Culture: 32; Dreamstime: Rik James, 45; iStockphoto: ivan-96, 19; Library of Congress: 4, 9, 15, 16, 17, 20, 22, 24, 26, 29, 33, 35, 39, 42, Manuscript Division, Abraham Lincoln Papers, 25, The Alfred Whital Stern Collection of Lincolniana, cover background and throughout; Newscom: Everett Collection, 37, Picture History, 30; North Wind Picture Archives: 36, 40; Shutterstock: Elena Shchipkova, 18, Everett Collection, 6, 10, 11, 14, 27, 28, 31, 41, Nigel Jarvis, 44, Volodymyr Nikitenko, 7; Smithsonian Institution: National Museum of American History / Transfer from Library of Congress, cover (bottom right), 1, 5, 43, National Portrait Gallery, transfer from the National Gallery of Art, gift of the A.W. Mellon Educational and Charitable Trust, 1942, 13; XNR Productions: 12, 23

Editorial Credits
Editor: Michelle Bisson; Designer: Tracy Davies; Media Researcher: Svetlana Zhurkin; Production Specialist: Tori Abraham

Smithsonian Credits
Barbara Clark Smith, Museum Curator, Division of Political, National Museum of American History; Bethanee Bemis, Museum Specialist, Division of Political History, National Museum of American History

TABLE OF CONTENTS

Words in **bold** are in the glossary.

Chapter 1
THE RIGHT TOOL, THE INKSTAND

All talented people need the right tool for their trade. A basketball player has a ball. A pianist has a piano. A painter has an easel. And a history-making president had an inkstand. Abraham Lincoln wrote one of this nation's most important documents with ink from an inkstand that became very important, itself.

Abraham Lincoln

4

Lincoln was president of the United States from 1861 to 1865. When Lincoln became president, the country was torn over the topic of slavery. Slavery in America was a system that allowed white people to force Black people to work for them for free. The first enslaved people had been brought to America from Africa in 1619 against their will.

The gradual outlawing of slavery was in place in the North by 1804, but it continued in the South. Southern states also wanted to make slavery legal in the new western areas. The Northern states did not agree. Neither did President Lincoln.

A Mysterious Tool

The inkstand President Lincoln used to write the Emancipation Proclamation is cloaked in mystery. No one knows where it came from or who first owned it. Lincoln himself didn't even own it. No one knows what other letters or telegrams were written with it. And no one can identify the animals carved on top of the inkwells. Some describe the animals as winged horses. But no one knows for sure.

A winged animal tops each of the two inkwells.

Angered by Lincoln's election, many Southern states **seceded** from the United States. They started their own government. They called themselves the Confederate States of America, or the Confederacy.

The Confederacy declared war against the rest of the United States, or the Union. This led to the American **Civil War** (1861–1865). The fighting ripped the nation apart.

Lincoln wanted to make a strong move to hopefully end the war and unite the country. As president, he had the power to do that. He decided to write an **executive order** that would free enslaved Southerners.

Many Black men fought in the Union military once they were no longer enslaved.

Lincoln used an ornately carved brass inkstand when writing the Emancipation Proclamation. The inkstand measured about 13 by 9 inches (33 by 20 centimeters). Two equally fancy inkwells sat upon it. This inkstand is now a historic **artifact**.

The Emancipation Proclamation freed many enslaved people. It turned the tide of the war. Many freed people joined the Union military. That greatly helped the Union army and hurt the Confederacy.

What made Lincoln decide to write the Emancipation Proclamation? To understand that, we need to travel back in time to Lincoln's beginnings.

What Is an Inkstand?

People used inkstands before they had ink-filled pens. An inkstand is a tray used to hold ink containers and a quill. A quill is a feather from a large bird. The narrow end of the quill is sharpened with a knife. The user would dip the quill into a container of ink. The ink would get sucked up the hollow part of the feather. The ink would come out the tip when pressed against paper.

An antique brass inkstand

Chapter 2
ABRAHAM LINCOLN'S BEGINNINGS

Lincoln's beginnings were humble. Few people would have guessed he would become a president. He was born on February 12, 1809. He grew up in a one-room log cabin. For most of his childhood, Lincoln's family lived on a farm in Indiana.

Lincoln spent less than a year in school as a boy. His father needed his help on the farm. But Lincoln loved to read. He sometimes walked miles to borrow books from friends and family. He also loved to tell stories. Reading helped him understand other points of view. It helped him grow up with a strong sense of honesty and fairness.

While Lincoln was growing up, he saw slavery firsthand, and he didn't like it. He didn't think it was right to own other people. Years later, when Lincoln became a great speaker, he often used quotes from his favorite books in his speeches against slavery.

As a boy, Lincoln spent many evenings reading by the fire.

FACT!
A U.S. holiday called Presidents' Day honors all U.S. presidents. It is held in February, the month Presidents George Washington and Abraham Lincoln were born.

Slavery in America began in 1619. Portuguese sailors had kidnapped and enslaved people in Africa. English pirates attacked the Portuguese and brought the captured Africans to the Jamestown Colony in present-day Virginia. Slavery allowed white people to own Black people. Enslaved people had no rights.

Enslaved people were made to work without pay in factories, on loading docks, and in homes. But most worked in farming. In the South, most enslaved people worked on large farms called plantations. They grew rice, tobacco, and cotton. Enslaved people were forced to do hard work in the hot sun.

The first enslaved people arriving as captives to colonial Jamestown in 1619

The Southern economy was based on the work of enslaved people. Plantation owners became rich because of the free labor.

By 1804, slavery was being gradually outlawed in Northern states. But it continued in the South. In 1808, bringing enslaved people from Africa was outlawed in the United States. But children born to enslaved women were enslaved at birth. Because of this, the internal slave trade continued in the South.

The Underground Railroad

The **Underground Railroad** was a collection of secret routes people used to escape slavery. Enslaved people fled the South for the Northern states and eventually Canada. No matter the route,

Escape attempts were often made at night under the cover of darkness.

it was a dangerous trip. It often involved walking or running hundreds of miles. People sometimes hid in swamps and didn't eat or rest for days. But for many, the chance for freedom made the danger worth it.

States that allowed slavery were known as slave states. Those that did not were called free states. There were disagreements between the two groups. Neither wanted the other to have more power in the **federal** government. In 1820, Missouri was admitted into the United States as a slave state. Because of this, Northerners demanded another free state. So Maine entered as a free state. This move was called the Missouri Compromise. It kept the peace for awhile.

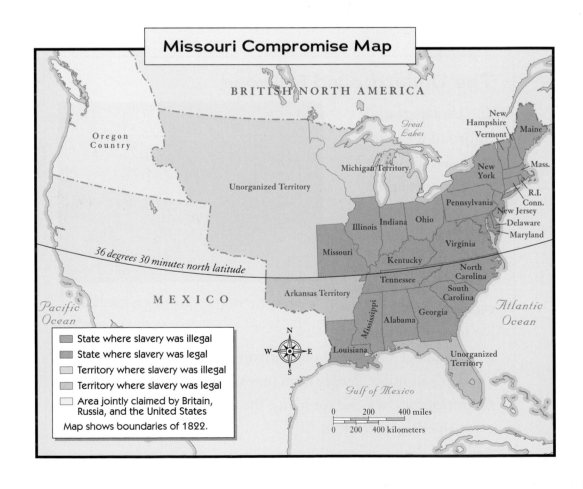

Missouri Compromise Map

- State where slavery was illegal
- State where slavery was legal
- Territory where slavery was illegal
- Territory where slavery was legal
- Area jointly claimed by Britain, Russia, and the United States

Map shows boundaries of 1822.

As part of the Missouri Compromise, leaders agreed that slavery was legal in the states south of Missouri and illegal north of it. But this agreement did not last forever.

The Missouri Compromise did not cover slavery in the western territories of the United States. Some people wanted to extend slavery into the new territories. Others did not want more slave states.

Senator Henry Clay introduced the bill for the Missouri Compromise.

Abraham Lincoln,
1858

Lincoln thought slavery would phase out gradually.
He was not an **abolitionist**. Abolitionists believed
all slavery should end immediately. At first, Lincoln
didn't think the federal government had the legal
power to end slavery where it already existed.

By 1858, Lincoln had tried many jobs. His desire
for equality and justice led him to politics. That year,
Lincoln ran for an Illinois seat in the U.S. Senate
against the current senator, Stephen Douglas.

Stephen Douglas,
early 1850s

    Lincoln and Douglas had seven famous debates
all over the state. Douglas believed slavery could
and should exist in the West. He proposed the
Kansas-Nebraska Act of 1854. This law would allow
white settlers of a new territory to decide whether
they wanted slavery in their new state by voting.
If passed, this act would likely overturn the balance
of free and slave states created with the Missouri
Compromise.

Lincoln began his Senate campaign with his famous "A House Divided" speech on June 16, 1858. In this speech he said, "A house divided against itself cannot stand." Lincoln was pointing out that eventually the United States would either need to be a place where everyone was free or where slavery was accepted.

Lincoln fought hard, but he lost. Douglas kept his seat. But Lincoln gained national attention. Many people thought he should run for president.

Dred and Harriet Scott

Dred and Harriet Scott were enslaved people who were married. Their owner moved them from Missouri to Illinois and the Wisconsin Territory, where slavery was not legal. The Scotts believed that since they had been taken to a free state, they should be freed. They sued for freedom. In 1857, the U.S. Supreme Court ruled against them. This decision angered many abolitionists. It also helped spark the Civil War.

Newspapers covered the Dred Scott case.

In 1860, Lincoln was chosen as the Republican candidate for president. Lincoln promised not to end slavery in the slave states. But he wanted to prevent it in the new western territories.

More people voted in the presidential election of 1860 than ever before. Lincoln received 39.8 percent of the vote and defeated three other candidates. He won all the Northern states except New Jersey and two western states, but not one Southern state. On March 4, 1861, Lincoln became the 16th President of the United States.

Abraham Lincoln was sworn in as President of the United States on March 4, 1861.

Chapter 3
LINCOLN AND THE CIVIL WAR

While Lincoln's supporters cheered the election results, many Southerners feared it. In the South, there was a growing distrust of the North. Southerners feared Lincoln would favor the Northern states and give them more power. They also thought Lincoln would try to end slavery in the United States. Doing that might destroy the South's economy.

Cotton was the most important crop in the South. It was in high demand around the world.

The South's economy was based on cotton. Cotton is a hard crop to harvest. It grows in a boll that is prickly and cuts skin. Southern plantation owners depended on enslaved people to plant and harvest the cotton.

Southern leaders also disagreed with Lincoln's hope to stop the spread of slavery. Southerners wanted to allow slavery in the western territories. An increase in slave-owning states would shift the balance of power in Washington in their favor.

The Cotton Gin

In 1794, Eli Whitney **patented** the cotton gin. The cotton gin greatly improved the process of removing seeds from cotton. It meant that cotton could be ready to sell more quickly. But to do that, Southern farmers needed more people to pick their cotton quickly. This gave them even more reason to expand slavery.

Eli Whitney's simple machine made removing cotton seeds easy.

By the time Lincoln took office in March 1861, seven Southern states had decided they no longer wanted to be part of the United States. South Carolina, Mississippi, Florida, Alabama, Georgia, Louisiana, and Texas formed the Confederate States of America. They made Jefferson Davis their president.

Confederates chose Jefferson Davis as their president because of his service in the Mexican War (1846–1848) and as Secretary of War under President Franklin Pierce.

On April 12, 1861, Confederate troops attacked Union troops at Fort Sumter, South Carolina. The Civil War had begun. Shortly after the attack, Virginia, Arkansas, Tennessee, and North Carolina left the Union and joined the Confederacy.

Four slave states stayed in the Union. These border states were Delaware, Maryland, Kentucky, and Missouri. Lincoln knew slavery was wrong, but he was determined to keep the country together. He allowed these states to continue slavery as long as they stayed loyal to the United States. This move was worth it to him to maintain the Union.

The issue of slavery tore friends and families apart. Many took opposing sides. In some cases brother fought brother. Before the war ended, more than 620,000 people would die.

> **FACT!**
> Robert Smalls was an enslaved man from South Carolina. He stole a Confederate ship and sailed North, narrowly avoiding capture. He gained his freedom and joined the U.S. Navy. Smalls later became a congressman.

As the war raged, Massachusetts senator Henry Wilson introduced a bill into Congress to end slavery in Washington, D.C. On April 16, 1862, President Lincoln signed the District of Columbia Compensated Emancipation Act. Signing this document freed enslaved people in Washington, D.C. But slavery was still legal in the loyal border states and in the South.

Henry Wilson

The United States During the Civil War

Many people thought the Civil War would end quickly. It did not. Both sides had advantages and disadvantages. The Union had twice as many soldiers as the Confederacy. The Union Army also had more money and weapons. Still, the Confederates had enslaved people to do hard labor. They carried equipment, dug trenches, cooked, and did other tasks. Confederate soldiers also had a deep passion to win the war. They believed their entire way of life was at stake. Despite the Union having more men, money, and weapons, the South won many battles.

Lincoln kept in touch with his commanders fighting on the front lines. Telephones had not yet been invented, so Lincoln used **telegraphs**. Telegraphs were the fastest way to send long-distance written messages called telegrams.

Telegraphs were expensive, and there weren't many of them. Lincoln did not have a telegraph in the White House. To use one, he had to walk to the War Department, about five minutes away. Lincoln spent a lot of his time in the telegraph office. He read telegrams about what was happening on the war front. He also used this time to write.

The United States War Department in the 1860s

Major Thomas Eckert was the chief of the telegraph office. A brass inkstand and two inkwells, all with detailed carvings, sat on Eckert's desk. And it was at that desk, using that inkstand, that Lincoln wrote the document that would change the course of U.S. history. That document was the Emancipation Proclamation.

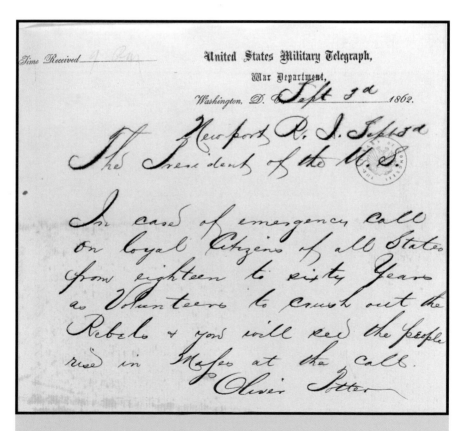

Once received by the telegraph office, messages were written down for the president to read.

Chapter 4
THE EMANCIPATION PROCLAMATION

Lincoln started his presidency with one main purpose—to keep the Union together. He saw the Confederates as a group of rebels. He did not see them as a new nation. Lincoln never referred to Jefferson Davis as president.

President Abraham Lincoln fought to keep the United States a unified nation.

Like many others, Lincoln thought the war would end quickly. But he was wrong. As the war dragged on, Lincoln knew he had to make a big move to end it.

Abolitionists believed slavery should be ended entirely. Now that the nation was at war, they argued, if Lincoln freed the enslaved people it would help the Union defeat the Confederacy. Enslaved people kept plantations going. Without them, the South's economy would crumble. The Confederacy would also lose any possible support from Europe. Europeans had already banned slavery in their countries. If the Union did too, these countries would side with them. Lincoln started to see the wisdom in this argument.

Enslaved people on a plantation in South Carolina prepare cotton for the cotton gin.

In July 1862, Congress passed a series of laws. They declared enslaved people free if they were enslaved by a Confederate military leader. They also said that Union soldiers were allowed to force Confederate enslavers to free their slaves. The laws even said that enslaved people who escaped would be considered free. Finally, the laws allowed Black men to work for and serve in the Union military. Most were made to do manual labor.

During the Second Battle of Bull Run, many enslaved people crossed the Rappahannok River to the Union side and to freedom.

At this time, Lincoln tried to gain freedom for enslaved people in border states. He offered the border state governors money to free enslaved people. But the governors chose to continue slavery instead of taking money from the federal government. That meant that, even though the Union government was freeing enslaved people in the South, those in the border states were still enslaved.

Frederick Douglass

Frederick Douglass escaped slavery in 1838. He became an author and an activist. He was one of the most important speakers of his time. Douglass and Lincoln agreed on freeing enslaved people. But Lincoln took longer to do it than Douglass had wanted. Douglass visited Lincoln in the White House three times in his life. On his second meeting, in 1864, Douglass and Lincoln discussed Lincoln's plan for emancipation. Douglass urged Lincoln to free all enslaved people, not just those in the Confederacy.

Frederick Douglass in 1864

Years of war had changed Lincoln's mind about who had the power to end slavery. He now believed that he could do it. Presidents have special powers during war. Lincoln decided to use this power to help the Union win the war and free more enslaved people.

In the summer of 1862, Lincoln sat at the desk with the inkstand in the War Department for a special purpose. He dipped his quill into the ink and began writing. This document would free the enslaved people in the Confederacy.

President Lincoln writing the Emancipation Proclamation in the telegraph office

Lincoln came back to the inkstand day after day to work on his document. He shared his first draft with his advisors on July 22, 1862. They urged him not to announce the Emancipation Proclamation immediately. They wanted to wait for a Union victory.

On September 17, 1862, at Antietam Creek in Maryland, the Union army stopped the Confederate advance. The Battle of Antietam was the victory Lincoln's advisors were waiting for.

President Lincoln and General George B. McClellan met in the general's tent after the Battle of Antietam.

On September 22, 1862, Lincoln announced the Emancipation Proclamation. It stated that enslaved people in any Confederate state were free unless that state returned to the Union before January 1, 1863. On that date, Lincoln signed the order into law.

The Emancipation Proclamation did not free the enslaved people in the border states. But it did turn the tide of war. Slavery had already ended in Britain and France. Up to this point, those countries had not taken sides. Most European countries still bought their cotton from the South. Now that the Union had taken a strong stand against slavery, these nations refused to trade with the Confederacy.

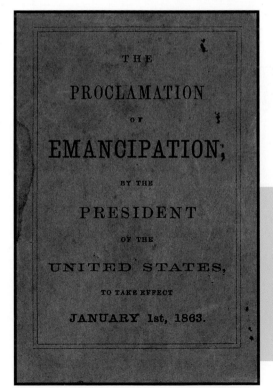

Booklets of the Emancipation Proclamation were printed for Union soldiers to hand out to enslaved people in the South.

Black Union soldiers charge into battle against
Confederate troops at Fort Wagner, South Carolina.

The Emancipation Proclamation also let Black men
join the Union military. About 200,000 did. These
Black servicemen fought bravely on the Union side.

The document also hurt the South's economy.
Many enslavers didn't tell enslaved people they were
legally free. But word still got around. As enslaved
people fled, Southern plantations had fewer workers.

Chapter 5
AFTER EMANCIPATION

Many people celebrated the Emancipation Proclamation. But it didn't end slavery. It only freed enslaved people in the Confederate states. It still had not freed those in the border states under Union control.

When the U.S. **Constitution** was created in 1787, slavery was legal in all 13 states. It wasn't mentioned in the Constitution. That left the phrase from the Declaration of Independence that "all men are created equal" up to others to define. In order to stop slavery throughout the country, the Constitution needed to be changed.

In April 1864, the U.S. Senate passed the 13th **Amendment** to the Constitution. It was meant to end slavery. But the order did not pass in the House of Representatives.

The House of Representatives was full of excitement when the 13th Amendment passed on January 31, 1865.

In November 1864, Lincoln was reelected. He worked tirelessly to create support for the 13th Amendment. It finally passed the House on January 31, 1865. Lincoln signed it the next day.

FACT!

The Syng Inkstand is another famous inkstand. It was made in 1752 by Philip Syng Jr. The Syng Inkstand was used to sign the Declaration of Independence in 1776 and the U.S. Constitution in 1787.

As slavery ended in the United States, so did the Civil War. On April 9, 1865, Confederate General Robert E. Lee surrendered to Union General Ulysses S. Grant. In four years, more than 10,000 armed conflicts and 50 major battles had been fought. At least 620,000 people died. Many more were injured. Now began the hard work of rebuilding the country.

The process of letting Southern states rejoin the Union was called **Reconstruction**. It lasted from 1865 to 1877.

Confederate General Robert E. Lee signs the papers to surrender to the Union forces.

Citizens in Charleston, South Carolina, take the loyalty oath to the Union in spring of 1865.

There were many debates on how to bring the country together. In the end, Southern states had to take two main steps. First, they had to swear loyalty to the United States of America. Second, they had to pay off their war debts.

All this time, the inkstand on which Lincoln had written the Emancipation Proclamation sat in the telegraph office of the War Department. No one thought it was anything remarkable. Events would soon change that.

Reconstruction was a long process. States were returning to the Union, but tensions still ran high. Lincoln talked with other leaders about Black men voting. Many white people who had enslaved Black people were furious about this idea. Some Southerners threatened to hurt Lincoln. His friends begged him to stay out of public places or to use armed guards. But Lincoln thought a president should not hide in the White House or behind guards.

Timeline of the Return to the Union of the 11 Confederate States

	State	Seceded from Union	Readmitted to Union
1.	South Carolina	Dec. 20, 1860	July 9, 1868
2.	Mississippi	Jan. 9, 1861	Feb. 23, 1870
3.	Florida	Jan. 10, 1861	June 25, 1868
4.	Alabama	Jan. 11, 1861	July 13, 1868
5.	Georgia	Jan. 19, 1861	July 15, 1870
6.	Louisiana	Jan. 26, 1861	July 9, 1868
7.	Texas	March 2, 1861	March 30, 1870
8.	Virginia	April 17, 1861	Jan. 26, 1870
9.	Arkansas	May 6, 1861	June 22, 1868
10.	North Carolina	May 20, 1861	July 4, 1868
11.	Tennessee	June 8, 1861	July 24, 1866

On April 14, 1865, President Lincoln and his wife went to see a play at Ford's Theatre in Washington, D.C. John Wilkes Booth, an actor and a Confederate sympathizer, snuck behind Lincoln and shot him. Lincoln died the next day. He was 56 years old.

Lincoln's death was tragic. But his legacy lived on. Months after he was killed, the United States adopted the 13th Amendment, on December 6, 1865. It ended slavery once and for all, throughout the nation.

John Wilkes Booth shot President Lincoln in the Presidential Box at Ford's Theatre.

With the Emancipation Proclamation and the passage of the 13th Amendment, slavery in the United States was over. More than four million Black people were no longer considered property. Many people agree that the ending of the Civil War and the signing of the 13th Amendment would not have been possible without the Emancipation Proclamation. This became Lincoln's legacy. It made the inkstand an important piece of history.

Many Black people left the South on riverboats heading to Northern states after the Civil War.

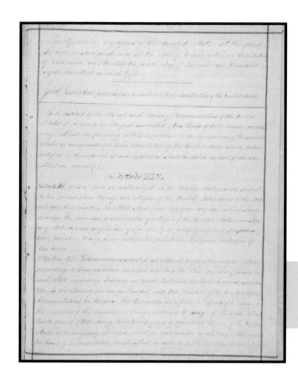

The 14th Amendment

In 1868, the 14th Amendment was another big step toward equality. It granted citizenship to all people born or **naturalized** in the United States. This meant that people who had once been enslaved were now U.S. citizens. They had the same rights under the law as white people.

Sadly, these legal changes did not end racism. Many white people still thought they were better than Black people. They found ways to put Black people down and made rules to hold them back. But they could no longer legally own them as property.

Chapter 6
THE INKSTAND TODAY

After Lincoln's death, the brass inkstand stayed on Major Eckert's desk until he gave it to Lincoln's family. Eckert had watched as the president had written the Emancipation Proclamation. He could tell by the president's focus that he was writing a document of great importance. He could not have known how important until years later. Lincoln's family eventually gave the inkstand to the Library of Congress. In 1962, the inkstand was moved to the Smithsonian, a group of museums and research centers in Washington, D.C.

Major Thomas Eckert in the 1860s

The Emancipation Proclamation inkstand

The Emancipation Proclamation inkstand is on display in the National Museum of American History (NMAC) in the American Democracy exhibit. In 2019, about 2.8 million people looked at the inkstand. Visitors to the museum stand less than a mile from the spot where Lincoln wrote his most important document. They can imagine that they are right there with him.

FACT!
The National Museum of African American History and Culture (NMAAHC) is entirely dedicated to African American life, history, and culture. Opened in 2016, it is the newest Smithsonian museum.

EXPLORE MORE

The National Museum of African American History and Culture

The National Museum of African American History and Culture

The National Museum of African American History and Culture is in downtown Washington, D.C. It has many exhibits to honor and teach about African American contributions throughout history. Exhibits include tributes to Black Americans in the arts, education, social change, sports, and more.

Abraham Lincoln Presidential Library

Lincoln's Presidential Library is located in Springfield, Illinois. In addition to its many books and exhibits, there are live historical performances. One is a re-creation of the president's assassination at Ford's Theatre as experienced by witnesses.

The Whitney Plantation

The Whitney Plantation in Louisiana shows what life was like for enslaved people on a sugarcane plantation in the late 1700s and early 1800s. Visitors can see the small shacks enslaved people had to live in. They can see the fields where enslaved people were forced to work long hours under the hot sun.

The old slave master's kitchen at the Whitney Plantation

GLOSSARY

abolitionist (ab-uh-LIH-shuhn-ist)—a person who worked to end slavery

amendment (uh-MEND-muhnt)—a change made to a law

artifact (AHR-tuh-fakt)—an important historical object

Civil War (SI-vil WOR)—(1861–1865) the battle between the North and the South to end slavery in the United States

constitution (kon-stuh-TOO-shuhn)—the laws stating the rights of the people and the powers of the government

executive order (ig-ZE-kyuh-tiv OR-dur)—a written instruction by the president that has the power of a federal law

federal (FED-ur-uhl)—relating to the national government

naturalize (NACH-ur-uh-lize)—to grant citizenship

patent (PAT-uhnt)—a legal document giving an inventor sole rights to make and sell an item he or she invented

Reconstruction (ree-kuhn-STRUHK-shuhn)—a period after the Civil War, when the U.S. government was rebuilding the Southern states

secede (suh-SEED)—to formally leave a group or an organization

telegraph (TEL-uh-graf)—a machine that uses electric signals to send messages called telegrams over long distances

Underground Railroad (UHN-dur-ground RAYL-rohd)—a system of helpful people and safe places for enslaved people who ran away during the mid-1800s

READ MORE

Jarrow, Gail. *Blood and Germs: The Civil War Battle Against Wounds and Disease.* New York: Calkins Creek, 2020.

Thompson, Ben. *Guts & Glory: The American Civil War.* New York: Little, Brown Books for Young Readers, 2015.

Van Lente, Fred. *Action Presidents #2: Abraham Lincoln!* New York: HarperAlley, 2020.

INTERNET SITES

Abraham Lincoln
si.edu/spotlight/abraham-lincoln

Abraham Lincoln Facts for Kids
kidzfeed.com/abraham-lincoln-facts-for-kids/

American Civil War: The Emancipation Proclamation
ducksters.com/history/emancipation_proclamation.php

INDEX